CW00517319

Hiking

JOURNAL

LET'S EXPLORE
THE WILD

Name : _____

Phone Number : _____

Emergency
Contact Name : _____

Phone Number : _____

Special request

Thank you for your trust. Your satisfaction means the world to me and I hope this hiking journal will meet your expectations.
I am a small independent author : if you enjoy this book, please take a few minutes to leave me a review on Amazon. Each one of your reviews is really important to support my work and help me provide you with new quality books.

Thank you !

Amy Birdwhistle

Hiking Journal & Log Book

© Copyright 2020 by Amy Birdwhistle. All rights reserved.

This publication is protected by copyright. No part of this book may be copied, reproduced or redistributed in any form without the express written consent and permission by the publisher.

TRAIL NAME

LOCATION

DATE

COMPANIONS

START TIME

END TIME

DURATION

DISTANCE

ALTITUDE

WEATHER CONDITIONS

🌡 ___   ☀️ ⛅ 🌧 ⛈ ❄️

🎐 ___   ☐ ☐ ☐ ☐ ☐

TERRAIN LEVEL

EASY   1   2   3   4   5   HARD
       ○   ○   ○   ○   ○

TRAIL TYPE

☐ LOOP	☐ ONE WAY
☐ OUT & BACK	☐ OTHERS

GEAR & EQUIPMENT

ANIMALS & PLANTS

THE HIKE

MILESTONE	TIME	NOTE

Hiking Notes

TRAIL NAME
LOCATION
DATE
COMPANIONS

WEATHER CONDITIONS

🌡 _____ ☀ ⛅ 🌧 ⛈ ❄

🌬 _____ ☐ ☐ ☐ ☐ ☐

START TIME
END TIME
DURATION
DISTANCE
ALTITUDE

TERRAIN LEVEL

EASY ○ 1 ○ 2 ○ 3 ○ 4 ○ 5 ○ HARD

TRAIL TYPE

☐ LOOP	☐ ONE WAY
☐ OUT & BACK	☐ OTHERS

GEAR & EQUIPMENT

ANIMALS & PLANTS

THE HIKE

MILESTONE	TIME	NOTE

Hiking Notes

🪧 TRAIL NAME
📍 LOCATION
📅 DATE
👥 COMPANIONS

WEATHER CONDITIONS

🌡️ _____   ☀️ ⛅ 🌧️ ⛈️ ❄️

🎏 _____   ☐ ☐ ☐ ☐ ☐

🚶 START TIME
🚩 END TIME
🧭 DURATION
📍 DISTANCE
⛰️ ALTITUDE

TERRAIN LEVEL

EASY ○ 1 ○ 2 ○ 3 ○ 4 ○ 5 ○ HARD

TRAIL TYPE

☐ LOOP	☐ ONE WAY
☐ OUT & BACK	☐ OTHERS

GEAR & EQUIPMENT

ANIMALS & PLANTS

THE HIKE

🗺️ MILESTONE	🕐 TIME	📝 NOTE

Hiking Notes

TRAIL NAME

LOCATION

DATE

COMPANIONS

START TIME

END TIME

DURATION

DISTANCE

ALTITUDE

WEATHER CONDITIONS

		☀	⛅	🌧	⛈	❄
🌡	___					
🚩	___	☐	☐	☐	☐	☐

TERRAIN LEVEL

EASY ○ — 1 ○ — 2 ○ — 3 ○ — 4 ○ — 5 ○ HARD

TRAIL TYPE

☐ LOOP	☐ ONE WAY
☐ OUT & BACK	☐ OTHERS

GEAR & EQUIPMENT

ANIMALS & PLANTS

THE HIKE

MILESTONE	TIME	NOTE

Hiking Notes

TRAIL NAME

LOCATION

DATE

COMPANIONS

START TIME

END TIME

DURATION

DISTANCE

ALTITUDE

WEATHER CONDITIONS

TERRAIN LEVEL

EASY 1 2 3 4 5 HARD

TRAIL TYPE

| ☐ LOOP | ☐ ONE WAY |
| ☐ OUT & BACK | ☐ OTHERS |

GEAR & EQUIPMENT

ANIMALS & PLANTS

THE HIKE

MILESTONE	TIME	NOTE

Hiking Notes

TRAIL NAME

LOCATION

DATE

COMPANIONS

START TIME

END TIME

DURATION

DISTANCE

ALTITUDE

WEATHER CONDITIONS

TERRAIN LEVEL

EASY   1   2   3   4   5   HARD

TRAIL TYPE

| ☐ LOOP | ☐ ONE WAY |
| ☐ OUT & BACK | ☐ OTHERS |

GEAR & EQUIPMENT

ANIMALS & PLANTS

THE HIKE

MILESTONE	TIME	NOTE

Hiking Notes

TRAIL NAME

LOCATION

DATE

COMPANIONS

START TIME

END TIME

DURATION

DISTANCE

ALTITUDE

WEATHER CONDITIONS

TERRAIN LEVEL

EASY 1 2 3 4 5 HARD

TRAIL TYPE

| ☐ LOOP | ☐ ONE WAY |
| ☐ OUT & BACK | ☐ OTHERS |

GEAR & EQUIPMENT

ANIMALS & PLANTS

THE HIKE

MILESTONE	TIME	NOTE

Hiking Notes

TRAIL NAME	WEATHER CONDITIONS

WEATHER CONDITIONS

Temperature: ___   ☀ ⛅ 🌧 ⛈ ❄

Wind: ___   ☐ ☐ ☐ ☐ ☐

TRAIL NAME

LOCATION

DATE

COMPANIONS

START TIME

END TIME

DURATION

DISTANCE

ALTITUDE

TERRAIN LEVEL

EASY ○——1 ○——2 ○——3 ○——4 ○——5 HARD

TRAIL TYPE

☐ LOOP	☐ ONE WAY
☐ OUT & BACK	☐ OTHERS

GEAR & EQUIPMENT

ANIMALS & PLANTS

THE HIKE

🗺 MILESTONE	🕐 TIME	📝 NOTE

Hiking Notes

TRAIL NAME	WEATHER CONDITIONS

LOCATION

DATE

COMPANIONS

TERRAIN LEVEL

EASY 1 2 3 4 5 HARD

TRAIL TYPE

☐ LOOP	☐ ONE WAY
☐ OUT & BACK	☐ OTHERS

START TIME

END TIME

DURATION

DISTANCE

ALTITUDE

GEAR & EQUIPMENT

ANIMALS & PLANTS

THE HIKE

🗺 MILESTONE	🕐 TIME	📝 NOTE

Hiking Notes

TRAIL NAME

LOCATION

DATE

COMPANIONS

START TIME

END TIME

DURATION

DISTANCE

ALTITUDE

WEATHER CONDITIONS

Temperature: ___

Wind: ___

☀ ⛅ 🌧 ⛈ ❄
☐ ☐ ☐ ☐ ☐

TERRAIN LEVEL

EASY 1 2 3 4 5 HARD

TRAIL TYPE

☐ LOOP   ☐ ONE WAY

☐ OUT & BACK   ☐ OTHERS

GEAR & EQUIPMENT

ANIMALS & PLANTS

THE HIKE

MILESTONE	TIME	NOTE

Hiking Notes

TRAIL NAME

LOCATION

DATE

COMPANIONS

START TIME

END TIME

DURATION

DISTANCE

ALTITUDE

WEATHER CONDITIONS

TERRAIN LEVEL

EASY 1 2 3 4 5 HARD

TRAIL TYPE

- [ ] LOOP
- [ ] ONE WAY
- [ ] OUT & BACK
- [ ] OTHERS

GEAR & EQUIPMENT

ANIMALS & PLANTS

THE HIKE

MILESTONE	TIME	NOTE

Hiking Notes

TRAIL NAME	
LOCATION	
DATE	
COMPANIONS	

WEATHER CONDITIONS

🌡 ___ ☀ ⛅ 🌧 ⛈ ❄

🚩 ___ ☐ ☐ ☐ ☐ ☐

START TIME	
END TIME	
DURATION	
DISTANCE	
ALTITUDE	

TERRAIN LEVEL

EASY 🌳 1 ○ 2 ○ 3 ○ 4 ○ 5 ○ 🏔 HARD

TRAIL TYPE

☐ LOOP	☐ ONE WAY
☐ OUT & BACK	☐ OTHERS

GEAR & EQUIPMENT

ANIMALS & PLANTS

THE HIKE

MILESTONE	TIME	NOTE

Hiking Notes

TRAIL NAME

LOCATION

DATE

COMPANIONS

START TIME

END TIME

DURATION

DISTANCE

ALTITUDE

WEATHER CONDITIONS

TERRAIN LEVEL

EASY 1 2 3 4 5 HARD

TRAIL TYPE

| ☐ LOOP | ☐ ONE WAY |
| ☐ OUT & BACK | ☐ OTHERS |

GEAR & EQUIPMENT

ANIMALS & PLANTS

THE HIKE

MILESTONE	TIME	NOTE

Hiking Notes

TRAIL NAME

LOCATION

DATE

COMPANIONS

START TIME

END TIME

DURATION

DISTANCE

ALTITUDE

WEATHER CONDITIONS

☀	⛅	🌧	⛈	❄
☐	☐	☐	☐	☐

TERRAIN LEVEL

EASY ○   1 ○   2 ○   3 ○   4 ○   5 ○   HARD

TRAIL TYPE

☐ LOOP	☐ ONE WAY
☐ OUT & BACK	☐ OTHERS

GEAR & EQUIPMENT

ANIMALS & PLANTS

THE HIKE

MILESTONE	TIME	NOTE

Hiking Notes

TRAIL NAME

LOCATION

DATE

COMPANIONS

START TIME

END TIME

DURATION

DISTANCE

ALTITUDE

WEATHER CONDITIONS

🌡 _____ ☀ ⛅ 🌧 ⛈ ❄

🎐 _____ ☐ ☐ ☐ ☐ ☐

TERRAIN LEVEL

EASY 1 2 3 4 5 HARD
○ ○ ○ ○ ○

TRAIL TYPE

| ☐ LOOP | ☐ ONE WAY |
| ☐ OUT & BACK | ☐ OTHERS |

GEAR & EQUIPMENT

ANIMALS & PLANTS

THE HIKE

MILESTONE	TIME	NOTE

Hiking Notes

TRAIL NAME

LOCATION

DATE

COMPANIONS

START TIME

END TIME

DURATION

DISTANCE

ALTITUDE

WEATHER CONDITIONS

☀ ⛅ 🌧 ⛈ ❄

☐ ☐ ☐ ☐ ☐

TERRAIN LEVEL

EASY ◯ 1 ◯ 2 ◯ 3 ◯ 4 ◯ 5 HARD

TRAIL TYPE

| ☐ LOOP | ☐ ONE WAY |
| ☐ OUT & BACK | ☐ OTHERS |

GEAR & EQUIPMENT

ANIMALS & PLANTS

THE HIKE

MILESTONE	TIME	NOTE

Hiking Notes

TRAIL NAME		WEATHER CONDITIONS

TRAIL NAME

LOCATION

DATE

COMPANIONS

START TIME

END TIME

DURATION

DISTANCE

ALTITUDE

WEATHER CONDITIONS

TERRAIN LEVEL

EASY 1 2 3 4 5 HARD

TRAIL TYPE

- ☐ LOOP
- ☐ ONE WAY
- ☐ OUT & BACK
- ☐ OTHERS

GEAR & EQUIPMENT

ANIMALS & PLANTS

THE HIKE

MILESTONE	TIME	NOTE

Hiking Notes

TRAIL NAME

LOCATION

DATE

COMPANIONS

START TIME

END TIME

DURATION

DISTANCE

ALTITUDE

WEATHER CONDITIONS

TERRAIN LEVEL

EASY 1 2 3 4 5 HARD

TRAIL TYPE

☐ LOOP		☐ ONE WAY	
☐ OUT & BACK		☐ OTHERS	

GEAR & EQUIPMENT

ANIMALS & PLANTS

THE HIKE

MILESTONE	TIME	NOTE

Hiking Notes

TRAIL NAME

LOCATION

DATE

COMPANIONS

START TIME

END TIME

DURATION

DISTANCE

ALTITUDE

WEATHER CONDITIONS

TERRAIN LEVEL

EASY 1 2 3 4 5 HARD

TRAIL TYPE

☐ LOOP	☐ ONE WAY
☐ OUT & BACK	☐ OTHERS

GEAR & EQUIPMENT

ANIMALS & PLANTS

THE HIKE

MILESTONE	TIME	NOTE

Hiking Notes

TRAIL NAME

LOCATION

DATE

COMPANIONS

START TIME

END TIME

DURATION

DISTANCE

ALTITUDE

WEATHER CONDITIONS

_____

_____

TERRAIN LEVEL

EASY 1   2   3   4   5 HARD

TRAIL TYPE

| ☐ LOOP | ☐ ONE WAY |
| ☐ OUT & BACK | ☐ OTHERS |

GEAR & EQUIPMENT

ANIMALS & PLANTS

THE HIKE

MILESTONE	TIME	NOTE

Hiking Notes

TRAIL NAME

LOCATION

DATE

COMPANIONS

START TIME

END TIME

DURATION

DISTANCE

ALTITUDE

WEATHER CONDITIONS

☐ ☐ ☐ ☐ ☐

TERRAIN LEVEL

EASY 1 2 3 4 5 HARD

TRAIL TYPE

☐ LOOP   ☐ ONE WAY

☐ OUT & BACK   ☐ OTHERS

GEAR & EQUIPMENT

ANIMALS & PLANTS

THE HIKE

MILESTONE	TIME	NOTE

Hiking Notes

	TRAIL NAME
	LOCATION
	DATE
	COMPANIONS

	START TIME
	END TIME
	DURATION
	DISTANCE
	ALTITUDE

WEATHER CONDITIONS

		☀	⛅	🌧	⛈	❄
	—	☐	☐	☐	☐	☐

TERRAIN LEVEL

EASY ○ — 1 ○ — 2 ○ — 3 ○ — 4 ○ — 5 ○ HARD

TRAIL TYPE

☐ LOOP	☐ ONE WAY
☐ OUT & BACK	☐ OTHERS

GEAR & EQUIPMENT

ANIMALS & PLANTS

THE HIKE

MILESTONE	TIME	NOTE

Hiking Notes

TRAIL NAME

LOCATION

DATE

COMPANIONS

START TIME

END TIME

DURATION

DISTANCE

ALTITUDE

WEATHER CONDITIONS

TERRAIN LEVEL

EASY 1 2 3 4 5 HARD

TRAIL TYPE

| ☐ LOOP | ☐ ONE WAY |
| ☐ OUT & BACK | ☐ OTHERS |

GEAR & EQUIPMENT

ANIMALS & PLANTS

THE HIKE

🗺 MILESTONE	🕐 TIME	📝 NOTE

Hiking Notes

TRAIL NAME

LOCATION

DATE

COMPANIONS

START TIME

END TIME

DURATION

DISTANCE

ALTITUDE

WEATHER CONDITIONS

☀️ ⛅ ☁️ ⛈️ ❄️

⬜ ⬜ ⬜ ⬜ ⬜

TERRAIN LEVEL

EASY 1 2 3 4 5 HARD

TRAIL TYPE

| ☐ LOOP | ☐ ONE WAY |
| ☐ OUT & BACK | ☐ OTHERS |

GEAR & EQUIPMENT

ANIMALS & PLANTS

THE HIKE

MILESTONE	TIME	NOTE

Hiking Notes

	TRAIL NAME
	LOCATION
	DATE
	COMPANIONS

	START TIME
	END TIME
	DURATION
	DISTANCE
	ALTITUDE

WEATHER CONDITIONS

		☀	⛅	🌧	⛈	❄
🌡	___					
🎏	___	☐	☐	☐	☐	☐

TERRAIN LEVEL

EASY 1 2 3 4 5 HARD
○ ○ ○ ○ ○

TRAIL TYPE

☐ LOOP	☐ ONE WAY
☐ OUT & BACK	☐ OTHERS

GEAR & EQUIPMENT

ANIMALS & PLANTS

THE HIKE

MILESTONE	TIME	NOTE

Hiking Notes

TRAIL NAME

LOCATION

DATE

COMPANIONS

START TIME

END TIME

DURATION

DISTANCE

ALTITUDE

WEATHER CONDITIONS

🌡 ——

🚩 ——

☀ ☁ ☁ ⛈ ❄

☐ ☐ ☐ ☐ ☐

TERRAIN LEVEL

EASY ○ 1 ○ 2 ○ 3 ○ 4 ○ 5 HARD

TRAIL TYPE

☐ LOOP   ☐ ONE WAY

☐ OUT & BACK   ☐ OTHERS

GEAR & EQUIPMENT

ANIMALS & PLANTS

THE HIKE

MILESTONE	TIME	NOTE

Hiking Notes

TRAIL NAME

LOCATION

DATE

COMPANIONS

START TIME

END TIME

DURATION

DISTANCE

ALTITUDE

WEATHER CONDITIONS

TERRAIN LEVEL

EASY 1 2 3 4 5 HARD

TRAIL TYPE

- [ ] LOOP
- [ ] ONE WAY
- [ ] OUT & BACK
- [ ] OTHERS

GEAR & EQUIPMENT

ANIMALS & PLANTS

THE HIKE

MILESTONE	TIME	NOTE

Hiking Notes

TRAIL NAME

LOCATION

DATE

COMPANIONS

START TIME

END TIME

DURATION

DISTANCE

ALTITUDE

WEATHER CONDITIONS

☐ ☐ ☐ ☐ ☐

TERRAIN LEVEL

EASY 1 2 3 4 5 HARD

TRAIL TYPE

☐ LOOP   ☐ ONE WAY

☐ OUT & BACK   ☐ OTHERS

GEAR & EQUIPMENT

ANIMALS & PLANTS

THE HIKE

MILESTONE	TIME	NOTE

Hiking Notes

TRAIL NAME

LOCATION

DATE

COMPANIONS

START TIME

END TIME

DURATION

DISTANCE

ALTITUDE

WEATHER CONDITIONS

TERRAIN LEVEL

EASY 1 2 3 4 5 HARD

TRAIL TYPE

☐ LOOP	☐ ONE WAY
☐ OUT & BACK	☐ OTHERS

GEAR & EQUIPMENT

ANIMALS & PLANTS

THE HIKE

MILESTONE	TIME	NOTE

Hiking Notes

TRAIL NAME

LOCATION

DATE

COMPANIONS

START TIME

END TIME

DURATION

DISTANCE

ALTITUDE

WEATHER CONDITIONS

🌡 _____   ☀ ⛅ ☁ 🌧 ❄

🚩 _____   ☐ ☐ ☐ ☐ ☐

TERRAIN LEVEL

EASY 1 ○ 2 ○ 3 ○ 4 ○ 5 ○ HARD

TRAIL TYPE

☐ LOOP	☐ ONE WAY
☐ OUT & BACK	☐ OTHERS

GEAR & EQUIPMENT

ANIMALS & PLANTS

THE HIKE

MILESTONE	TIME	NOTE

Hiking Notes

🪧 TRAIL NAME		**WEATHER CONDITIONS**

🌡 _____   ☀ ⛅ ☁ ⛈ ❄

🚩 _____   ☐ ☐ ☐ ☐ ☐

📍 **LOCATION**

📅 **DATE**

👥 **COMPANIONS**

TERRAIN LEVEL

EASY 1 ○ 2 ○ 3 ○ 4 ○ 5 ○ HARD

🥾 **START TIME**

🚩 **END TIME**

⏱ **DURATION**

📍 **DISTANCE**

⛰ **ALTITUDE**

TRAIL TYPE

☐ LOOP	☐ ONE WAY
☐ OUT & BACK	☐ OTHERS

GEAR & EQUIPMENT

ANIMALS & PLANTS

THE HIKE

📍 MILESTONE	🕐 TIME	📝 NOTE

Hiking Notes

TRAIL NAME

LOCATION

DATE

COMPANIONS

START TIME

END TIME

DURATION

DISTANCE

ALTITUDE

WEATHER CONDITIONS

TERRAIN LEVEL

EASY 1 2 3 4 5 HARD

TRAIL TYPE

☐ LOOP	☐ ONE WAY
☐ OUT & BACK	☐ OTHERS

GEAR & EQUIPMENT

ANIMALS & PLANTS

THE HIKE

MILESTONE	TIME	NOTE

Hiking Notes

TRAIL NAME

LOCATION

DATE

COMPANIONS

START TIME

END TIME

DURATION

DISTANCE

ALTITUDE

WEATHER CONDITIONS

TERRAIN LEVEL

	1	2	3	4	5	
EASY	○	○	○	○	○	HARD

TRAIL TYPE

☐ LOOP		☐ ONE WAY	
☐ OUT & BACK		☐ OTHERS	

GEAR & EQUIPMENT

ANIMALS & PLANTS

THE HIKE

MILESTONE	TIME	NOTE

Hiking Notes

TRAIL NAME

LOCATION

DATE

COMPANIONS

START TIME

END TIME

DURATION

DISTANCE

ALTITUDE

WEATHER CONDITIONS

TERRAIN LEVEL

	1	2	3	4	5	
EASY	○	○	○	○	○	HARD

TRAIL TYPE

☐ LOOP	☐ ONE WAY
☐ OUT & BACK	☐ OTHERS

GEAR & EQUIPMENT

ANIMALS & PLANTS

THE HIKE

MILESTONE	TIME	NOTE

Hiking Notes

TRAIL NAME

LOCATION

DATE

COMPANIONS

START TIME

END TIME

DURATION

DISTANCE

ALTITUDE

WEATHER CONDITIONS

TERRAIN LEVEL

| EASY | 1 | 2 | 3 | 4 | 5 | HARD |

TRAIL TYPE

| ☐ LOOP | ☐ ONE WAY |
| ☐ OUT & BACK | ☐ OTHERS |

GEAR & EQUIPMENT

ANIMALS & PLANTS

THE HIKE

MILESTONE	TIME	NOTE

Hiking Notes

TRAIL NAME

LOCATION

DATE

COMPANIONS

START TIME

END TIME

DURATION

DISTANCE

ALTITUDE

WEATHER CONDITIONS

🌡 ———

🚩 ———

☐ ☐ ☐ ☐ ☐

TERRAIN LEVEL

EASY 1 2 3 4 5 HARD
○   ○   ○   ○   ○

TRAIL TYPE

| ☐ LOOP | ☐ ONE WAY |
| ☐ OUT & BACK | ☐ OTHERS |

GEAR & EQUIPMENT

ANIMALS & PLANTS

THE HIKE

MILESTONE	TIME	NOTE

Hiking Notes

TRAIL NAME

LOCATION

DATE

COMPANIONS

START TIME

END TIME

DURATION

DISTANCE

ALTITUDE

WEATHER CONDITIONS

🌡 ——

🚩 ——

☀ ⛅ 🌧 ⛈ ❄

☐ ☐ ☐ ☐ ☐

TERRAIN LEVEL

EASY 1 2 3 4 5 HARD
○ ○ ○ ○ ○

TRAIL TYPE

| ☐ LOOP | ☐ ONE WAY |
| ☐ OUT & BACK | ☐ OTHERS |

GEAR & EQUIPMENT

ANIMALS & PLANTS

THE HIKE

MILESTONE	TIME	NOTE

Hiking Notes

TRAIL NAME

LOCATION

DATE

COMPANIONS

START TIME

END TIME

DURATION

DISTANCE

ALTITUDE

WEATHER CONDITIONS

		☀	⛅	🌧	⛈	❄
🌡	___					
🚩	___	☐	☐	☐	☐	☐

TERRAIN LEVEL

EASY — 1 — 2 — 3 — 4 — 5 — HARD
○ ○ ○ ○ ○

TRAIL TYPE

☐ LOOP	☐ ONE WAY
☐ OUT & BACK	☐ OTHERS

GEAR & EQUIPMENT

ANIMALS & PLANTS

THE HIKE

MILESTONE	TIME	NOTE

Hiking Notes

TRAIL NAME

LOCATION

DATE

COMPANIONS

START TIME

END TIME

DURATION

DISTANCE

ALTITUDE

WEATHER CONDITIONS

🌡 _____ ☀ ⛅ ☁ ⛈ ❄

🚩 _____ ☐ ☐ ☐ ☐ ☐

TERRAIN LEVEL

EASY 1 ○ 2 ○ 3 ○ 4 ○ 5 ○ HARD

TRAIL TYPE

☐ LOOP   ☐ ONE WAY

☐ OUT & BACK   ☐ OTHERS

GEAR & EQUIPMENT

ANIMALS & PLANTS

THE HIKE

MILESTONE	TIME	NOTE

Hiking Notes

TRAIL NAME

LOCATION

DATE

COMPANIONS

START TIME

END TIME

DURATION

DISTANCE

ALTITUDE

WEATHER CONDITIONS

TERRAIN LEVEL

	1	2	3	4	5	
EASY	○	○	○	○	○	HARD

TRAIL TYPE

☐ LOOP	☐ ONE WAY
☐ OUT & BACK	☐ OTHERS

GEAR & EQUIPMENT

ANIMALS & PLANTS

THE HIKE

MILESTONE	TIME	NOTE

Hiking Notes

TRAIL NAME

LOCATION

DATE

COMPANIONS

START TIME

END TIME

DURATION

DISTANCE

ALTITUDE

WEATHER CONDITIONS

TERRAIN LEVEL

| EASY | 1 | 2 | 3 | 4 | 5 | HARD |

TRAIL TYPE

- [ ] LOOP
- [ ] ONE WAY
- [ ] OUT & BACK
- [ ] OTHERS

GEAR & EQUIPMENT

ANIMALS & PLANTS

THE HIKE

MILESTONE	TIME	NOTE

Hiking Notes

TRAIL NAME

LOCATION

DATE

COMPANIONS

START TIME

END TIME

DURATION

DISTANCE

ALTITUDE

WEATHER CONDITIONS

TERRAIN LEVEL

	1	2	3	4	5	
EASY	○	○	○	○	○	HARD

TRAIL TYPE

☐ LOOP	☐ ONE WAY
☐ OUT & BACK	☐ OTHERS

GEAR & EQUIPMENT

ANIMALS & PLANTS

THE HIKE

MILESTONE	TIME	NOTE

Hiking Notes

TRAIL NAME

LOCATION

DATE

COMPANIONS

START TIME

END TIME

DURATION

DISTANCE

ALTITUDE

WEATHER CONDITIONS

TERRAIN LEVEL

EASY 1 2 3 4 5 HARD

TRAIL TYPE

☐ LOOP ☐ ONE WAY

☐ OUT & BACK ☐ OTHERS

GEAR & EQUIPMENT

ANIMALS & PLANTS

THE HIKE

MILESTONE	TIME	NOTE

Hiking Notes

TRAIL NAME

LOCATION

DATE

COMPANIONS

START TIME

END TIME

DURATION

DISTANCE

ALTITUDE

WEATHER CONDITIONS

☀ ⛅ ☁ ⛈ ❄

TERRAIN LEVEL

| EASY | 1 | 2 | 3 | 4 | 5 | HARD |

TRAIL TYPE

| ☐ LOOP | ☐ ONE WAY |
| ☐ OUT & BACK | ☐ OTHERS |

GEAR & EQUIPMENT

ANIMALS & PLANTS

THE HIKE

MILESTONE	TIME	NOTE

Hiking Notes

TRAIL NAME

LOCATION

DATE

COMPANIONS

START TIME

END TIME

DURATION

DISTANCE

ALTITUDE

WEATHER CONDITIONS

🌡 —

🚩 —

☀ ⛅ 🌧 ⛈ ❄

☐ ☐ ☐ ☐ ☐

TERRAIN LEVEL

EASY	1	2	3	4	5	HARD
○	○	○	○	○		

TRAIL TYPE

☐ LOOP	☐ ONE WAY
☐ OUT & BACK	☐ OTHERS

GEAR & EQUIPMENT

ANIMALS & PLANTS

THE HIKE

MILESTONE	TIME	NOTE

Hiking Notes

TRAIL NAME

LOCATION

DATE

COMPANIONS

START TIME

END TIME

DURATION

DISTANCE

ALTITUDE

WEATHER CONDITIONS

		☀	⛅	🌧	⛈	❄
🌡	____					
🚩	____	☐	☐	☐	☐	☐

TERRAIN LEVEL

EASY ○ 1 ○ 2 ○ 3 ○ 4 ○ 5 HARD

TRAIL TYPE

☐ LOOP	☐ ONE WAY
☐ OUT & BACK	☐ OTHERS

GEAR & EQUIPMENT

ANIMALS & PLANTS

THE HIKE

MILESTONE	TIME	NOTE

Hiking Notes

TRAIL NAME

LOCATION

DATE

COMPANIONS

START TIME

END TIME

DURATION

DISTANCE

ALTITUDE

WEATHER CONDITIONS

☀️ ⛅ 🌧️ ⛈️ ❄️
☐ ☐ ☐ ☐ ☐

TERRAIN LEVEL

EASY	1	2	3	4	5	HARD
○	○	○	○	○		

TRAIL TYPE

☐ LOOP   ☐ ONE WAY

☐ OUT & BACK   ☐ OTHERS

GEAR & EQUIPMENT

ANIMALS & PLANTS

THE HIKE

MILESTONE	TIME	NOTE

Hiking Notes

TRAIL NAME

LOCATION

DATE

COMPANIONS

START TIME

END TIME

DURATION

DISTANCE

ALTITUDE

WEATHER CONDITIONS

TERRAIN LEVEL

EASY 1 2 3 4 5 HARD

TRAIL TYPE

| ☐ LOOP | ☐ ONE WAY |
| ☐ OUT & BACK | ☐ OTHERS |

GEAR & EQUIPMENT

ANIMALS & PLANTS

THE HIKE

MILESTONE	TIME	NOTE

Hiking Notes

TRAIL NAME

LOCATION

DATE

COMPANIONS

START TIME

END TIME

DURATION

DISTANCE

ALTITUDE

WEATHER CONDITIONS

TERRAIN LEVEL

EASY 1 2 3 4 5 HARD

TRAIL TYPE

| ☐ LOOP | ☐ ONE WAY |
| ☐ OUT & BACK | ☐ OTHERS |

GEAR & EQUIPMENT

ANIMALS & PLANTS

THE HIKE

MILESTONE	TIME	NOTE

Hiking Notes

TRAIL NAME

LOCATION

DATE

COMPANIONS

START TIME

END TIME

DURATION

DISTANCE

ALTITUDE

WEATHER CONDITIONS

| 🌡 ____ | ☀ | ⛅ | 🌧 | ⛈ | ❄ |
| 🚩 ____ | ☐ | ☐ | ☐ | ☐ | ☐ |

TERRAIN LEVEL

| EASY | 1 ○ | 2 ○ | 3 ○ | 4 ○ | 5 ○ | HARD |

TRAIL TYPE

| ☐ LOOP | ☐ ONE WAY |
| ☐ OUT & BACK | ☐ OTHERS |

GEAR & EQUIPMENT

ANIMALS & PLANTS

THE HIKE

🗺 MILESTONE	🕐 TIME	📝 NOTE

Hiking Notes

Printed in Great Britain
by Amazon

73024332R00061